|| "Dedicated to all who seek to understand and appreciate Indian culture and tradition." ||

Contents

Contents

Prayer

"Om Bhadram Karnebhih Shrunuyaama
DevaahBhadram Pashyemaakshabhiryajatraah
SthirairangaistushtuvaamsastanoobhihVyashema
Devahitam YadaayuhSwasti Na Indro
VridhashravaahSwasti Nah Pooshaa
VishwavedaahSwasti Nastaarkshyo ArishtanemihSwasti
No Brihaspatir DadhaatuOm Shantih, Shantih, Shantih"

The literal meaning of this mantra is: OM. O Gods! Let us
hear auspicious words from our ears. O reverent Gods! Let
us behold propitious visions from our eyes, let our organs
and body be stable, healthy, and strong. Let us do that
which is pleasing to the gods in the life span allotted to us.
May Indra, inscribed in the scriptures, bring us fortune!
May Pushan, the knower of the world, grant us prosperity!
May Trakshya, who vanquishes enemies, bestow us with
blessings! May Brihaspati bring us success!
OM Peace, Peace, Peace.

ॐ ॐ ॐ

About The Author

Dr. Jagadeesh Pillai is a renowned Guinness World Record holder, writer, and researcher hailing from Varanasi, also known as the abode of Lord Shiva. With a Ph.D. in Vedic Science and a range of creative ideas and achievements, he is a true polymath. He is the author of more than 100 books including Research Publications. Although his roots can be traced back to Kerala, the people of Varanasi hold him in high regard and affectionately consider him one of their own.

Dr. Pillai has achieved four Guinness World Records in the following subjects:

"Script to Screen" - In this record, Dr. Pillai produced and directed an animation film within the shortest time possible, breaking the previous record set by Canadians. He has also received numerous national and international awards and recognitions for this achievement.

Longest Line of Postcards - For this record, Dr. Pillai created a line of 16,300 postcards on the occasion of the 163rd anniversary of Indian Postal Day. The event also included a questionnaire about the Indian flag.

Largest Poster Awareness Campaign - Dr. Pillai designed an awareness campaign on the subject of "Beti Bachao - Beti Padhao" (Save the Girl Child - Educate the Girl Child) to achieve this record.

Largest Envelope - In tribute to the Indian Prime Minister's

"Make in India" initiative, Dr. Pillai created a 4000 square meter envelope using waste paper to achieve this record.

Attempted - **70000 Candles on a 210 kg Cake** - To celebrate the 70th Indian Independence Day, Dr. Pillai attempted to light 70,000 candles on a 210 kg cake, which was recorded in World Records India.

Attempted - **Documentary on Dhamek Stupa of Sarnath in 17 Languages** - Dr. Pillai attempted to create a documentary on the Dhamek Stupa of Sarnath, dubbing it in 17 different languages. The result of this attempt is currently awaiting confirmation from the Guinness World Records.

Dr. Pillai is skilled in teaching the Bhagavad Gita, a Hindu scripture, and is popular among young people. He has helped many young people improve their lives through his motivational teachings.

In addition to teaching, he has composed and sung numerous Sanskrit Bhajans and patriotic songs.

He has also written and directed several short films and documentaries for awareness campaigns, and has volunteered with the police in both UP and Kerala to spread awareness about various issues through videos and photography.

Incredibly, he has produced and directed over 100 documentaries about the city of Varanasi, all on his own.

He has also helped and guided more than 25 boys and girls to achieve world records through creative and innovative methods. He is a multifaceted person who uses his intellect and the blessings given to him by God to excel in various areas. He is both a teacher and a student, always learning and teaching, and is able to master any subject he comes across.

He is a selfless social activist and motivational speaker who has overcome struggles and failures to become a successful and enthusiastic individual with a rich life experience.

In addition to his work with the Bhagavad Gita, he is also an efficient Tarot card reader, Astro-Vastu consultant, and a talented singer and composer. He has sung the entire Ram Charita Manas and Bhagavad Gita in his own compositions, and has sung the phrase "Lokah Samastha Sukhino Bhavantu" in 50 different languages. He is currently working on a detailed and scientific study of Vedas, Upanishads, Puranas, and the Bhagavad Gita. He has also composed and sung the Hanuman Chalisa and Gayatri Mantra in 108 and 1008 different compositions, respectively.

Awards - Four Times Guinness World Records, Winner of Mahatma Gandhi Vishwa Shanti Puraskar, Mahatma Gandhi Global Peace Ambassador, Kashi Ratna Award, Dr. APJ Abdul Kalam Motivational Person of the Year 2017, Mother Teresa Award, Indira Gandhi Priyadarshini Award, Bharat Vikas Ratna Award, Udyog Ratna Award, Vigyan Prasar Award, Poorvanchal Ratn Samman.

ツツツ

Preface

India is a land of ancient spiritual traditions and a rich cultural heritage. From the grand temples of the south to the ashrams of the north, the country is home to a vast array of spiritual landmarks that have attracted seekers of enlightenment for thousands of years. This book, "From Temples to Ashrams: A Guide to the Spiritual Landmarks of India," is a comprehensive guide to the most significant and inspiring spiritual destinations in India.

The book begins with an overview of the history and development of Indian spirituality, tracing its roots back to the Vedic era and highlighting the major spiritual movements and figures that have shaped the country's religious landscape. The reader will learn about the ancient practices of yoga and meditation, as well as the beliefs and customs of the various Hindu and Buddhist sects that have flourished in India.

The book then delves into a detailed exploration of the many spiritual landmarks of India, including the grand temples of South India, such as the Meenakshi Temple in Madurai and the Sri Ranganathaswamy Temple in Srirangam. The reader will also discover the sacred caves of Ajanta and Ellora, the ancient city of Varanasi, and the ashrams of the north, such as the Sri Aurobindo Ashram in Pondicherry and the Parmarth Niketan in Rishikesh.

In addition to providing a detailed guide to these spiritual landmarks, the book also includes practical information on how to plan your visit, including tips on transportation, accommodations, and local customs. Whether you are a seasoned traveler or a first-time visitor to India, this book will help you make the most of your spiritual journey.

The book is not only a guide but also an inspiration, as it provides a deeper understanding of the spiritual and cultural significance of these landmarks, and the significance of their teachings in the current era. It will also help readers to connect with the people and places they encounter, and to gain a deeper appreciation of India's rich spiritual heritage.

"From Temples to Ashrams: A Guide to the Spiritual Landmarks of India" is an essential guide for anyone interested in exploring the spiritual and cultural heritage of India. It is a comprehensive, informative, and inspiring guide that will help you to make the most of your spiritual journey and deepen your understanding of the ancient practices and beliefs that have shaped this fascinating country.

ᏢᏢᏢ

ONE

THE ROOTS OF INDIAN SPIRITUALITY: A HISTORICAL OVERVIEW

The roots of Indian spirituality can be traced back to the Vedic era, which lasted from approximately 1500 BCE to 500 BCE. During this time, the ancient Indian sages, known as rishis, composed a collection of sacred texts known as the Vedas. These texts, which include the Rigveda, Yajurveda, Samaveda and Atharvaveda, contain hymns, prayers, and mantras that were used in rituals and ceremonies to worship the gods. The Vedas also contain the earliest known references to yoga and meditation, which were seen as ways to achieve union with the divine.

As the Vedic era came to a close, a new spiritual movement emerged that was centered around the concept of renunciation. This movement, known as Jainism and Buddhism, was founded by Mahavira and Gautama Buddha respectively. Both of these teachings emphasized the importance of non-violence, self-control, and the attainment of spiritual liberation through the elimination of desire and attachment. This movement rejected the caste system and the ritualism of Vedic tradition and paved the way for the development of new spiritual practices and beliefs.

Another significant spiritual movement that emerged in India during this time was the Bhakti movement. This movement, which began in the 7th century CE, emphasized the importance of devotion to a personal god and the importance of love and devotion in the spiritual path. Bhakti movement also provided a new way of religious expression, that is not limited to the caste system, and it was embraced by people from all walks of life. This movement gave rise to many saints and poets such as Kabir, Ravidas, and Tukaram, who sang the praises of their chosen deity in a language that was understood by the common people.

As the Bhakti movement evolved, it gave rise to many new sects and sub-sects such as the vaishnavism, shaktism and shaivism, each with its own unique practices and beliefs. These sects further developed the Bhakti movement and made it more accessible to the masses.

In conclusion, Indian spirituality has a rich and diverse history that has been shaped by many different spiritual movements and figures. The Vedic era laid the foundation for the development of yoga and meditation, while the Jainism and Buddhism rejected the caste system and the ritualism of the Vedic tradition and provided a new way of religious expression. The Bhakti movement, with its emphasis on devotion and love, further developed Indian spirituality and made it more accessible to the masses. These movements and figures have all contributed to the rich tapestry of Indian spirituality that we see today.

"India is a land of ancient wisdom and modern innovation, where tradition and modernity coexist in perfect harmony." - Goldie Hawn

TWO

INTRODUCTION TO THE SACRED LANDMARKS OF INDIA: THE SIGNIFICANCE OF SPIRITUAL PLACES IN INDIA

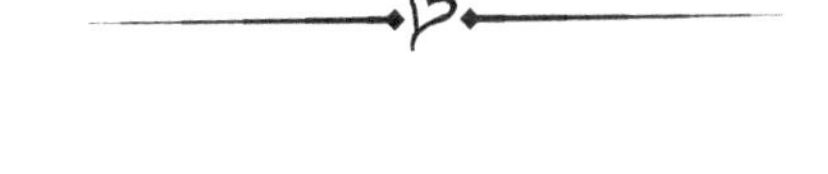

India is a land of ancient spiritual traditions and a rich cultural heritage. The country is home to a vast array of spiritual landmarks that have attracted seekers of enlightenment for thousands of years. From grand temples to sacred caves, ancient cities to ashrams, these spiritual places have played an important role in shaping the religious and cultural landscape of India.

The spiritual landmarks of India are not just places of worship but also hold great historical, cultural and architectural significance. They are also considered to be an embodiment of the deep-seated spiritual beliefs of the people of India. Many of these landmarks have been in existence for centuries and have been visited by countless pilgrims over the years.

The grand temples of South India are architectural marvels, adorned with intricate carvings and sculptures, and are considered to be some of the most beautiful spiritual landmarks in the country. The caves of Ajanta and Ellora, which date back to the 2nd century BCE, are known for their intricate rock-cut architecture and frescoes depicting Buddhist, Jain and Hindu stories. The ancient city of Varanasi, situated on the banks of the River Ganges, is considered to be one of the most sacred places in Hinduism and is visited by thousands of pilgrims every year.

The ashrams of the north, such as the Sri Aurobindo Ashram in Pondicherry and the Parmarth Niketan in Rishikesh, have been attracting spiritual seekers for decades. These ashrams provide a place for individuals to live and practice spiritual disciplines such as meditation, yoga, and self-inquiry. They also offer an opportunity for individuals to immerse themselves in the spiritual practices and teachings of the ashram, and provide a window into the spiritual traditions of India.

The spiritual landmarks of India are not just places of worship but also hold great historical, cultural and architectural significance. They are an embodiment of the deep-seated spiritual beliefs of the people of India, and are an essential part of the country's religious and cultural heritage. This chapter will provide an overview of the significance of these spiritual places in India and how they reflect the rich spiritual heritage of the country.

❦❦❦

"India is a country of many languages and many religions, but it is also a country of many beautiful landscapes and many beautiful buildings." - Gustave Flaubert

THREE

THE GREAT TEMPLE CITIES OF SOUTH INDIA: A GUIDE TO THE MOST FAMOUS TEMPLE TOWNS LIKE MADURAI, THANJAVUR, AND KANCHIPURAM

South India is home to some of the most famous temple towns in the country, which are known for their grand temples, intricate carvings, and rich cultural heritage. Some of the most notable temple towns in South India include Madurai, Thanjavur, and Kanchipuram. These temple towns are considered to be architectural marvels and are an important part of the religious and cultural heritage of South India.

Madurai is known for its Meenakshi Temple, which is one of the most famous temples in South India and is dedicated to the goddess Meenakshi, an incarnation of the goddess Parvati. The temple is known for its impressive architecture and intricate carvings, which include 14 gopurams (gateway towers) and thousands of statues of gods and goddesses. It's also an important pilgrimage site for Hindus and is visited by thousands of pilgrims every year.

Thanjavur is home to the Brihadeeswarar Temple, which is another architectural wonder of South India and is dedicated to Lord Shiva. The temple was built in the 11th century CE by Raja Raja Chola, one of the greatest kings of the Chola dynasty. The temple is known for its impressive architecture and is considered to be one of the greatest examples of Chola architecture.

Kanchipuram, also known as the city of thousand temples, is an ancient city which is famous for its many temples, including the famous Kailasanathar Temple and the Ekambareswarar Temple. These temples are considered to be some of the most beautiful and significant spiritual landmarks in the country, and are known for their intricate carvings and sculptures.

The great temple cities of South India like Madurai,

Thanjavur, and Kanchipuram are a must-visit for anyone interested in exploring the architectural and cultural heritage of India. These temple towns are home to some of the most famous and beautiful temples in the country, which are known for their grand architecture, intricate carvings, and rich cultural heritage. They also serve as an important pilgrimage site for Hindus and are visited by thousands of devotees every year. This chapter provides a guide to the most famous temple towns of South India and an overview of the temples, their history and significance in the spiritual and cultural heritage of the region.

ppp

"India has a way of mesmerizing you,
captivating you, and fascinating you. There's a
magic to India that's hard to explain." -
Anthony Bourdain

FOUR

Exploring the Cave Temples of India

India is a land of many natural and architectural wonders. One of the most captivating features of the country's landscape are its various ancient cave temples. These temples are not only awe-inspiring in their grandeur and grandiose, but they are also windows into India's rich and ancient cultural heritage.

The country has been home to many dynasties, such as the Mauryan Dynasty and the Chalukya Dynasty, and each have left behind intricate and intricate caves that have been hewn out of rocks and hillsides. These caves have provided shelter to many monks and ascetics over the centuries and have become important pilgrimage sites for many sects of Hinduism.

The cave temples of India are a marvel of ancient

architecture and art. These caves, carved out of solid rock, are not only architectural wonders but also hold great historical and religious significance.

One of the most famous cave temples in India is the Elephanta Caves, located on Elephanta Island in the state of Maharashtra. These caves date back to the 6th century AD and are dedicated to the Hindu god, Lord Shiva. The caves are known for their intricate carvings and sculptures, including a 20-foot-tall statue of Lord Shiva, known as the Trimurti.

Another famous cave temple complex is the Ajanta Caves, located in the state of Maharashtra. These caves date back to the 2nd century BC and are known for their beautiful frescoes and rock-cut architecture. The Ajanta Caves were designated as a UNESCO World Heritage Site in 1983. These are some of the world's oldest surviving monuments and were carved out of the rock between the 2nd century BCE and the 6th century CE. The Ajanta Cave paintings are some of the earliest examples of Buddhist art and were significant at the time for their movement away from the more stylistic paintings of earlier eras.

The Ellora Caves, located in the state of Maharashtra, are another set of ancient cave temples in India. These caves date back to the 5th century AD and are known for their beautiful carvings and sculptures that depict scenes from Buddhism, Hinduism, and Jainism. The Ellora Caves were also designated as a UNESCO World Heritage Site in 1983. The stunning carvings and intricate details of the temple show the skilled craftsmanship that went into the building of these structures and how the artisans were able to seamlessly blend religious themes and art within the cave walls.

The Badami Cave Temples are another incredible cave temple complex located in Karnataka, India. This series of four temples was built between the 6th and 8th centuries survive in near perfect condition and boast ancient inscriptions and artworks. The inner walls and pillars of the temples are examples of exquisite craftsmanship and grace and reveal some of the earliest forms of Indian art.

The Udayagiri and Khandagiri Caves, located near Bhubaneswar in Orissa, are another important series of ancient cave temples. The double hills of these caves offer a spectacular view of the city skyline and were the site of many important religious festivals and gatherings. The caves, dating back to the 2nd century BCE, also feature several intricately carved sculptures and friezes depicting different Hindu gods and goddesses from the era.

These ancient cave temples not only remind us of the grandeur of the architectures of the past, but also represent a unique window into India's cultural heritage. From the intricate stone carvings to the ancient inscriptions, these temples are marvels of human ingenuity and a reminder of the powerful influence that religion can have on culture.

Visiting these ancient cave temples is a journey back in time, giving visitors a glimpse into the rich cultural heritage of India and the skill of ancient Indian architects and artists.

❧❧❧

"India is a land of ancient civilization and culture, where tradition and modernity coexist in perfect harmony." - Dalai Lama

FIVE

THE HIMALAYAN MYSTICS: EXPLORING THE ASHRAMS AND SPIRITUAL CENTERS IN THE HIMALAYAS

The Himalayas have long been considered a sacred mountain range and have been a destination for spiritual seekers for centuries. The ashrams and spiritual centers in the Himalayas offer an opportunity for individuals to immerse themselves in the spiritual practices and teachings of the region, and provide a window into the spiritual traditions of India. These ashrams and centers are situated in some of the most picturesque and serene settings, providing an ideal environment for spiritual growth and self-discovery.

One of the most famous ashrams in the Himalayas is the Parmarth Niketan Ashram, located in Rishikesh. The ashram is considered to be one of the largest and most renowned ashrams in India, and offers a wide range of spiritual programs and activities, including yoga and meditation classes, devotional singing, and lectures on spiritual teachings. The ashram also has a beautiful Ganga Aarti ceremony every evening, which is considered to be one of the most beautiful and spiritual experiences in Rishikesh.

Another famous ashram in the Himalayas is the Sivananda Ashram, located in Uttarkashi. The ashram is known for its yoga and meditation classes, and for its emphasis on selfless service, simplicity, and devotion to God. The ashram also offers a range of courses and retreats on yoga and spiritual development, making it a popular destination for spiritual seekers.

In addition to ashrams, there are also many spiritual centers in the Himalayas, such as the Osho International Meditation Resort in Pune and the Sri Sri Ravi Shankar Ashram in Bangalore. These centers offer a variety of spiritual practices and teachings, including meditation, yoga, and self-inquiry.

The ashrams and spiritual centers in the Himalayas are an important part of the spiritual heritage of India. These centers offer an opportunity for individuals to immerse themselves in the spiritual practices and teachings of the region, and provide a window into the spiritual traditions of India. The ashrams and centers in the Himalayas are situated in some of the most picturesque and serene settings, providing an ideal environment for spiritual growth and self-discovery. This chapter provides an overview of the famous ashrams and spiritual centers in the Himalayas, their teachings and practices, and how they reflect the spiritual heritage of the region.

"India is the meeting place of the religions and among these Hinduism alone is by itself a vast and complex thing, not so much a religion as a great diversified and yet subtly unified mass of spiritual thought, realization and aspiration."
- Sri Aurobindo

SIX

THE JYOTIRLINGA TEMPLES: A GUIDE TO THE 12 MOST FAMOUS SHIVA TEMPLES IN INDIA

The Jyotirlinga temples, also known as the lingam of light, are a group of 12 most famous and sacred temples dedicated to Lord Shiva in India. These temples are considered to be the most sacred shrines of Lord Shiva and are believed to be the places where Lord Shiva revealed his divine power to the world. These temples are widely revered and are considered to be an important part of the religious and cultural heritage of India.

The twelve Jyotirlinga temples are:
Somnath Temple in Gujarat

**Mallikarjuna Temple in Andhra Pradesh
Mahakaleshwar Temple in Madhya Pradesh
Omkareshwar Temple in Madhya Pradesh
Kedarnath Temple in Uttarakhand
Bhimashankar Temple in Maharashtra
Kashi Vishwanath Temple in Uttar Pradesh
Trimbakeshwar Temple in Maharashtra
Vaidyanath Temple in Jharkhand
Nageshwar Temple in Gujarat
Rameshwar Temple in Tamil Nadu
Grishneshwar Temple in Maharashtra**

Each of these temples has its own unique history and significance. The Somnath Temple, for example, is considered to be the first Jyotirlinga temple and is believed to have been built by Lord Soma, the Moon God. The Mallikarjuna Temple, on the other hand, is considered to be one of the most powerful Jyotirlinga temples and is believed to have been built by Lord Shiva himself.

Visiting these temples is considered to be an important pilgrimage for many Hindus, and devotees often visit all 12 temples in a single trip as a part of the Jyotirlinga darshan. These temples are also known for their grand architecture and intricate carvings, and many of them are considered to be architectural marvels.

The Jyotirlinga Temples are a group of 12 most famous and sacred temples dedicated to Lord Shiva in India. These temples are considered to be the most sacred shrines of Lord Shiva and are an important part of the religious and cultural heritage of India. Each of these temples has its own unique history and significance and visiting these temples is considered to be an important pilgrimage for many Hindus. This chapter provides a guide to the 12 Jyotirlinga Temples, their history and significance, and how they reflect the spiritual heritage of India.

ϡϡϡ

"In India, I found a race of mortals living upon the Earth, but not adhering to it." - Ralph Waldo Emerson

SEVEN

THE VAISHNAVITE HOLY PLACES: A GUIDE TO THE MOST FAMOUS VISHNU TEMPLES AND PILGRIMAGE SITES IN INDIA

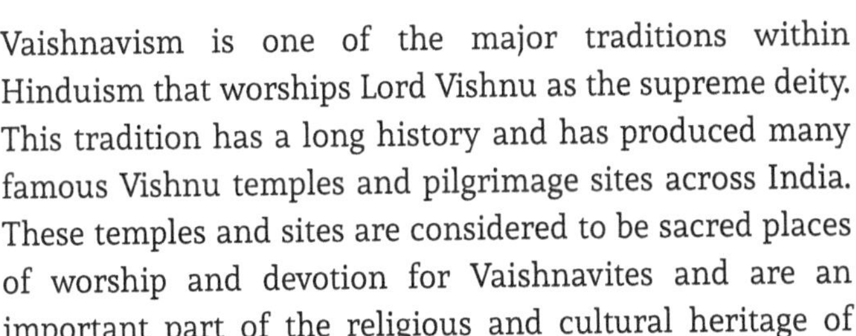

Vaishnavism is one of the major traditions within Hinduism that worships Lord Vishnu as the supreme deity. This tradition has a long history and has produced many famous Vishnu temples and pilgrimage sites across India. These temples and sites are considered to be sacred places of worship and devotion for Vaishnavites and are an important part of the religious and cultural heritage of

India.

Some of the most famous Vishnu temples and pilgrimage sites include:

Sri Ranganathaswamy Temple in Srirangam, Tamil Nadu

Lord Jagannath Temple in Puri, Odisha

Lord Venkateswara Temple in Tirumala, Andhra Pradesh

Sri Venkateswara Temple in Pandharpur, Maharashtra

Shrinathji Temple in Nathdwara, Rajasthan

ISKCON Temple in Delhi

Shri Nathji Temple in Vrindavan, Uttar Pradesh

Lord Ranganatha Swamy Temple in Melkote, Karnataka

These temples and sites are not only considered to be sacred places of worship but also hold great historical and architectural significance. The Sri Ranganathaswamy Temple in Srirangam, for example, is considered to be one of the most important Vaishnavite temples in South India and is known for its impressive architecture. The Lord Jagannath Temple in Puri is also an important pilgrimage site and is known for its grand chariot festival, the Rath Yatra. The Lord Venkateswara Temple in Tirumala is one of the most visited pilgrimage sites in India, and is known for its wealth and grandeur.

Visiting these temples and pilgrimage sites is considered to be an important pilgrimage for many Vaishnavites and many devotees often visit all of these sites in a single trip as a part of the Vaishnavite darshan. These temples and sites are also known for their grand architecture and intricate carvings, and many of them are considered to be architectural marvels.

The Vaishnavite Holy Places are an important part of the religious and cultural heritage of India. These temples and pilgrimage sites are considered to be sacred places of worship and devotion for Vaishnavites and are an important part of the religious and cultural heritage of India. This chapter provides a guide to the most famous Vishnu temples and pilgrimage sites in India, their history and significance, and how they reflect the spiritual heritage of the Vaishnavite tradition. Some of the most famous temples and pilgrimage sites include the Sri Ranganathaswamy Temple in Srirangam, Lord Jagannath Temple in Puri, Lord Venkateswara Temple in Tirumala, and ISKCON Temple in Delhi. These temples and sites are not only considered to be sacred places of worship but also hold great historical and architectural significance. Visiting these temples and pilgrimage sites is considered to be an important pilgrimage for many Vaishnavites, and many devotees often visit all of these sites in a single trip as a part of the Vaishnavite darshan. They also offer an opportunity for individuals to immerse themselves in the spiritual practices and teachings of the Vaishnavite tradition and offer an insight into the spiritual heritage of India.

ॐॐॐ

"India is a land where the mind is without fear and the head is held high." - Rabindranath Tagore

EIGHT

THE ANCIENT STUPAS AND MONASTERIES: THE MOST FAMOUS BUDDHIST PILGRIMAGE SITES IN INDIA

Buddhism has a rich history in India and has produced many famous pilgrimage sites across the country. These sites are considered to be sacred places of worship and devotion for Buddhists and are an important part of the religious and cultural heritage of India. Some of the most famous Buddhist pilgrimage sites include:

Bodh Gaya: where the Buddha attained enlightenment under the Bodhi tree.

Sarnath: where the Buddha delivered his first sermon

Sanchi: the site of the Great Stupa, one of the oldest stone structures in India.

Ajanta and Ellora caves: known for their rock-cut architecture and frescoes depicting Buddhist stories.

Kushinagar: where the Buddha attained parinirvana

Lalitgiri, Ratnagiri, and Udayagiri: three of the earliest Buddhist monasteries in Odisha.

Dhamek Stupa in Sarnath, Uttar Pradesh

Mahabodhi Temple in Bodh Gaya, Bihar

These pilgrimage sites are not only considered to be sacred places of worship but also hold great historical, architectural and archaeological significance. The Bodh Gaya, for example, is considered to be the most important Buddhist pilgrimage site and is known for its association with the Buddha's attainment of enlightenment. The Ajanta and Ellora caves are also known for their intricate rock-cut architecture and frescoes depicting Buddhist stories. Visiting these pilgrimage sites is considered to be an important pilgrimage for many Buddhists and many devotees often visit all of these sites in a single trip as a part of the Buddhist darshan.

The Ancient Stupas and Monasteries are an important part of the religious and cultural heritage of India. These pilgrimage sites are considered to be sacred places of worship and devotion for Buddhists and are an important part of the religious and cultural heritage of India. This chapter provides a guide to the most famous Buddhist pilgrimage sites in India, their history and significance, and how they reflect the spiritual heritage of the Buddhist tradition. These pilgrimage sites offer an opportunity for individuals to immerse themselves in the spiritual practices and teachings of the Buddhist tradition and offer an insight into the spiritual heritage of India.

ppp

"India is a land of wonder, a land of mystery, a land of inspiration." - David Lean

Spiritual Wanderlust: Exploring the lesser-known spiritual places of India

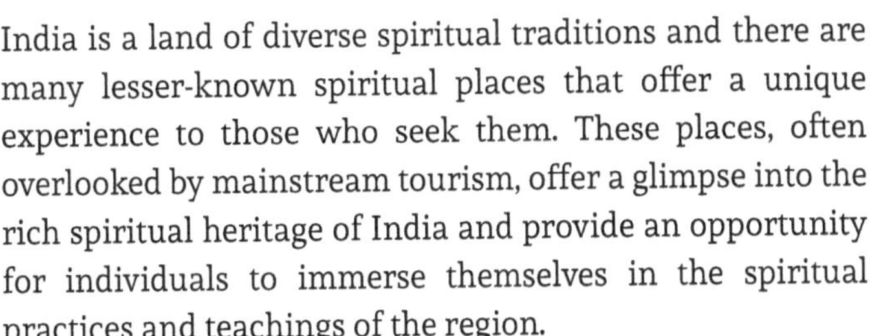

India is a land of diverse spiritual traditions and there are many lesser-known spiritual places that offer a unique experience to those who seek them. These places, often overlooked by mainstream tourism, offer a glimpse into the rich spiritual heritage of India and provide an opportunity for individuals to immerse themselves in the spiritual practices and teachings of the region.

Some of the lesser-known spiritual places in India include:

The Khajuraho Temples in Madhya Pradesh, known for their erotic sculptures and architectural wonder.

The Ajmer Sharif Dargah in Rajasthan, a Sufi shrine dedicated to the famous Sufi saint Moinuddin Chishti

The Pashupatinath Temple in Nepal, one of the most sacred temples dedicated to Lord Shiva and a UNESCO World Heritage Site.

The Kollur Mookambika Temple in Karnataka, dedicated to the goddess Mookambika and considered to be one of the seven Mukti Sthalas.

The Haridwar and Rishikesh in Uttarakhand, known as the gateway to the Himalayas and a place of spiritual significance for Hindus.

The Chidambaram Temple in Tamil Nadu, dedicated to Lord Nataraja, the cosmic dancer and considered one of the five elements of the universe.

The Sabarimala Temple in Kerala, dedicated to Lord Ayyappa and one of the most visited pilgrimage sites in India.

The Ganges River, considered sacred by Hindus and is known for its many ghats and temples along its banks.

These places are not only known for their spiritual significance but also hold great historical, architectural and cultural significance. They offer an opportunity to explore the rich spiritual heritage of India and to experience the unique spiritual practices and teachings of the region.

India is a land of diverse spiritual traditions and there are many lesser-known spiritual places that offer a unique experience to those who seek them. These places, often overlooked by mainstream tourism, offer a glimpse into the rich spiritual heritage of India and provide an opportunity for individuals to immerse themselves in the spiritual practices and teachings of the region. This chapter provides a guide to the lesser-known spiritual places of India, their history and significance and how they reflect the spiritual heritage of India.

❦❦❦

"The beauty of India is that it is a land of contrasts. It is not just one color, it is not just one smell, it is not just one tradition." - A.R. Rahman

TEN

VARANASI: THE CITY OF LIGHT

Varanasi, also known as Benares or Kashi, is one of the oldest continuously inhabited cities in the world and is considered one of the most sacred places in Hinduism. The city is situated on the banks of the River Ganges and is considered to be a spiritual capital of India. The city is known for its many temples, ghats (stone steps leading to the river), and ashrams, which attract thousands of pilgrims from all over the world.

Varanasi has a rich history dating back to the 11th century BCE. The city is believed to have been founded by Lord Shiva and is considered to be one of the seven sacred cities in Hinduism. The city is also an important center for Buddhism and Jainism, as it was an important center of learning and pilgrimage during the time of the Buddha.

The city is known for its many temples, the most famous of which is the Kashi Vishwanath Temple, which is dedicated to Lord Shiva. The temple is considered to be one of the most sacred temples in Hinduism and is visited by thousands of pilgrims every year. Other notable temples in the city include the Durga Temple, the Sankat Mochan Temple, and the Annapoorna Devi Temple.

The ghats of Varanasi are also an important part of the city's spiritual significance. There are more than 100 ghats in Varanasi, and each one has its own unique history and significance. The most famous of the ghats is the Manikarnika Ghat, which is considered to be one of the most sacred places in Hinduism. Pilgrims come to this ghat to bathe in the Ganges and perform rituals for the dead.

The city is also home to many ashrams and spiritual centers, such as the Parmarth Niketan and the Sivananda Ashram, which provide spiritual teachings and yoga classes to visitors.

Defenitely, Varanasi is a city steeped in spiritual significance and history. The city's temples, ghats, and ashrams attract thousands of pilgrims from all over the world and provide a glimpse into the rich spiritual heritage of India. The city is considered to be one of the most sacred places in Hinduism and is a must-visit destination for anyone interested in exploring the spiritual side of India.

ᎶᎶᎶ

"India is the cradle of the human race, the birthplace of human speech, the mother of history, the grandmother of legend, and the great grandmother of tradition." - Mark Twain

ELEVEN

The Ashrams of the North

Ashrams are spiritual communities that provide a place for individuals to live and practice spiritual disciplines such as meditation, yoga, and self-inquiry. The ashrams of the north, such as the Sri Aurobindo Ashram in Pondicherry and the Parmarth Niketan in Rishikesh, have been attracting spiritual seekers for decades. These ashrams are considered to be some of the most renowned and respected spiritual communities in India and provide a window into the spiritual traditions of the country.

The Sri Aurobindo Ashram, located in Pondicherry, is a spiritual community that was founded by Sri Aurobindo and the Mother in 1926. The Ashram is based on the teachings of Sri Aurobindo, who believed that true spiritual development involves the integration of the spiritual and the material. The Ashram offers a variety of programs and activities such as yoga, meditation, and self-inquiry, which are designed to help individuals integrate their spiritual and material lives.

The Parmarth Niketan, located in Rishikesh, is one of the largest ashrams in India and is considered to be a spiritual hub for many spiritual seekers. The ashram offers a variety of programs and activities, including yoga and meditation classes, devotional singing, and lectures on spiritual teachings. The ashram also has a beautiful Ganga Aarti ceremony every evening, which is considered to be one of the most beautiful and spiritual experiences in Rishikesh.

Both of these ashrams also provide accommodation and facilities for visitors, who can stay in the ashram to immerse themselves in the spiritual practices and teachings. Both the ashrams also have a strong focus on self-inquiry, service and oneness, which is a holistic approach to spiritual growth.

The ashrams of the north, such as the Sri Aurobindo Ashram in Pondicherry and the Parmarth Niketan in Rishikesh, provide a window into the spiritual traditions of India. These ashrams offer a variety of programs and activities that are designed to help individuals integrate their spiritual and material lives and to provide an opportunity for self-inquiry and spiritual growth. These ashrams have been attracting spiritual seekers for decades and continue to be a popular destination for those looking to deepen their spiritual practice.

ÞÞÞ

"India is not a country, it is a continent." - Rabindranath Tagore

TWELVE

TEMPLES OF SOUTH INDIA: A TOUR OF ARCHITECTURAL WONDERS

The temples of South India are renowned for their grand architecture and intricate carvings, and they are considered to be some of the most beautiful and significant spiritual landmarks in the country. Some of the most famous temples in South India include the Meenakshi Temple in Madurai, the Sri Ranganathaswamy Temple in Srirangam, and the Brihadeeswarar Temple in Thanjavur. These temples are not only architectural wonders but also important religious and cultural heritage sites that reflect the rich religious and cultural heritage of the region.

The Meenakshi Temple, located in Madurai, is one of the most famous temples in South India and is dedicated to the goddess Meenakshi, an incarnation of the goddess Parvati. The temple is known for its impressive architecture and intricate carvings, which include 14 gopurams (gateway towers) and thousands of statues of gods and goddesses. The temple is also an important pilgrimage site for Hindus and is visited by thousands of pilgrims every year.

The Sri Ranganathaswamy Temple, located in Srirangam, is one of the most important Vaishnavite temples in South India and is dedicated to Lord Ranganatha, an incarnation of Lord Vishnu. The temple is known for its impressive architecture and is considered to be one of the largest temple complexes in the world. The temple complex includes 21 gopurams, 50 shrines, and 39 pavilions, making it an architectural wonder.

The Brihadeeswarar Temple, located in Thanjavur, is another architectural wonder of South India and is dedicated to Lord Shiva. The temple was built in the 11th century CE by Raja Raja Chola, one of the greatest kings of the Chola dynasty. The temple is known for its impressive architecture and is considered to be one of the greatest examples of Chola architecture.

The temples of South India are architectural wonders that reflect the rich religious and cultural heritage of the region. These temples, such as the Meenakshi Temple in Madurai, the Sri Ranganathaswamy Temple in Srirangam, and the Brihadeeswarar Temple in Thanjavur, not only offer an opportunity to marvel at the intricate architecture but also offer an insight into the religious and cultural heritage of the region. These temples are also important pilgrimage sites for Hindus and are visited by thousands of pilgrims every year.

❧❧❧

Reference

|| Internet, Scriptures and Books from Libraries ||

• 67 •

Other Books Of The Author

1. The Moments When I Met God
2. Kashiyile Theertha Pathangal
3. GURU GYAN VANI
4. Abhiprerak Gita
5. ASSI SE JAIN GHAT TAK
6. Hopelessness of Arjuna
7. The Soul and It's True Nature
8. Sense of Action (Karma)
9. Action through Wisdom
10. Action through Wisdom
11. THEORY AND PRACTICAL OF EVERY ACTION
12. LOGICAL UNDERSTANDING OF THE SUPREME
13. THE IMPERISHABLE SUPREME
14. Yatra Nishadraj se Hanuman Ghat Tak
15. Yatra Karnatak Ghat se Raja Ghat Tak
16. Yatra Pandey Ghat se Prayagraj Ghat Tak
17. Yatra Ranjendra Prasad Ghat se Dattatreya Ghat Tak
18. YaatraSindhiya Ghat se Gwaliar Ghat Tak
19. Yatra Mangala Gauri Ghat se Hanuman Gadhi Ghat Tak
20. Yatra Gaay Ghat Se Nishad Ghat Tak
21. MAA GANGA, GHATEN EVM UTSAV
22. Ganga Arti Dev Deepavali evam Any Utsav
23. Potentials of Digitalized India
24. VEDIC CONSCIOUSNESS
25. A Brief Introduction to Vedic Science
26. Kashi ke Barah Jyotirling
27. IMPACT OF MOTIVATION
28. Let's have a Milky Way Journey
29. Color Therapy in a Nutshell

30. Rigveda in a Nutshell
31. Yajurveda in a Nutshell
32. Samveda in a Nutshell
33. Atharva Veda in a Nutshell
34. Ayushman Bhava - Ayurveda
35. Srimad Bhagavad Gita and Upanishad Connection
36. Srimad Bhagavad Gita - an attempt to summarize each chapter.
37. Facts and Impact of Nakshatra
38. Astro Gems - NAVARATNA
39. Ekadashi - A Concise Overview
40. A Concise View of Hanuman Chalisa
41. Inspirational Gita
42. Nakshatraranyam
43. Summary of 18 Mahapuranas
44. Synopsis of 18 Upa Puranas
45. Rigvediya Upanishads
46. Shukla Yajurvediya Upanishads
47. Krishna Yajurvediya Upanishads
48. Samavediya Upanishads
49. Atharvavediya Upanishads
50. The Seven Great Sages
51. From Rocket Scientist to President Dr. APJ Abdul Kalam
52. The Visionary's Voice - Quotes of Dr. APJ Abdul Kalam
53. The Wisdom of Swami Vivekananda: Insights and Inspiration from a Legendary Spiritual Teacher
54. Ayurvedic Remedies from the Garden
55. Sages and Seers
56. Rising Strong – Motivational Stories of Women
57. Beyond Flames -Mystery stories of Funeral Ghat Manikarnika
58. The Origins of Tulsi: A Look at the Mythological Roots of the Plant"

ppp

Contact

DR. JAGADEESH PILLAI

PhD in Vedic Science

Four Times Guinness World Record Holder

Winner of Mahatma Gandhi Vishwa Shanti Puraskar and
Global Peace Ambassador

Gemology, Astro & Vastu Consultant - Spiritual Counselor

Consultant for designing World Record Ideas

Efficient Tarot Card Reader

9839093003

myrichindia@gmail.com

drjagadeeshpillai@facebook

drjagadeeshpillai@instagram

jagadeeshpillai@youtube

www. JAGADEESHPILLAI.com

ᎮᎮᎮ

www.ingramcontent.com/pod-product-compliance
Lightning Source LLC
Chambersburg PA
CBHW050746180726
48003CB00020B/1936